HEALTH & Diet

Healthy Lifestyles

BY GEMMA MCMULLEN

BookLife
King's Lynn
Norfolk PE30 4LS

ISBN: 978-1-78637-092-1

All rights reserved.
Printed in Malaysia.

©This edition was published in
2018. First published in 2017.

Written by:
Gemma McMullen

Edited by:
Grace Jones

Designed by:
Natalie Carr

LOOK FOR THE WORDS LIKE **THIS** IN THE GLOSSARY ON PAGE 31.

Contents

DO YOU KNOW THE FIVE FOOD GROUPS? FIND OUT INSIDE ON PAGE 7.

WHAT DO YOU KNOW ABOUT YOUR DIGESTIVE SYSTEM? FEATURED ON PAGE 20.

HEALTHY

HEALTHY BODY

The way that we treat our bodies is extremely important because without good health we would **CEASE** to exist. The food that we eat and the amount that we exercise, both contribute massively to the health of our bodies. We need to respect our bodies so that they stay healthy for longer.

WHAT IS HEALTHY LIVING?

ALTHOUGH WE ARE ALL UNIQUE, OUR BODIES ALL WORK IN THE SAME WAY AND NEED THE SAME THINGS TO STAY HEALTHY.

HEALTHY living is the term given to the ideal way of living our lives. Put simply, it means that we live our lives in the healthiest way possible. Healthy living relates to every single aspect of our lives, from the things that we eat to the amount that we sleep.

Living

HEALTHY CHOICES

It is unlikely that we will always choose the healthiest option, but it is important that we have the correct information so we are able to make **INFORMED CHOICES** about the way we live our lives. This book is about exercise and the ways in which it contributes to a healthy lifestyle.

HEALTHY MIND

The health of our minds is of equal importance to that of our bodies. Our minds control the way that we think and the ways in which we use our bodies. Keeping a healthy mind includes having healthy relationships with others and being able to deal with our problems rationally.

WHY DO WE NEED TO *Eat?*

STAYING ALIVE!

WITHOUT food, we would not be able to survive. Food provides our bodies with the energy they need to breathe, think, move and keep warm. The food that we eat helps us to grow and to stay healthy. We need to eat plenty of food in order to keep going.

CARBOHYDRATES

PROTEIN

THE BALANCED PLATE

The five food groups are: proteins, which largely consist of meat, poultry and fish; carbohydrates, which include foods such as bread, pasta and cereal; fruits and vegetables; sugar and dairy. You should try to eat food from every group at every meal. The Balanced Plate is split into a pie chart so that you can see what proportion of each food types you should eat.

HEALTHY FOOD

FRUITS AND VEGETABLES

The types of food that we eat impact on the ways that our bodies work; the healthier the food is, the healthier our bodies will be. Different foods effect us in different ways. It is important that we eat foods from all of the five food groups to achieve a balanced diet.

DAIRY

SUGAR

NO SINGLE FOOD INCLUDES ALL OF THE NUTRIENTS THAT THE BODY NEEDS, SO IT IS IMPORTANT THAT WE EAT A BALANCED DIET

Proteins

AS WITH ALL FOODS, THE WAY THAT WE **COOK MEAT** CAN EFFECT HOW HEALTHY IT IS.

FOOD THAT IS **FRIED** IS NOT AS GOOD FOR US AS FOOD THAT IS GRILLED.

HEALTHY PROTEINS

To have a balanced diet, we all need to eat protein. Some sources of protein are better for our bodies than others. White meats and fish have a much lower fat content than red meats. Because of this, it is better to eat white meat and fish more regularly than red meat.

MEATS AND FISH

WE get meat and fish from the bodies of animals. They are an important part of our diets because they contain proteins which our bodies need. Proteins are good for us as they help the body to grow and be able to repair itself. As well as eating the meat of animals, we also eat animal products, such as eggs. Eggs are a good source of protein. Our muscles and organs are all made out of protein.

UNHEALTHY PROTEINS

Processed meat is meat that has been altered so it will last longer. Processed foods are generally not very good for us, so we should only eat them in small quantities. Ready meals often include processed meats. It is always better to cook your own food from scratch rather than eat a ready meal.

MANY STUDIES
HAVE SHOWN THAT
VEGETARIANS
WHO EAT A WELL-BALANCED DIET ARE
HEALTHIER
THAN MEAT-EATERS.

VEGETARIANS: FOR THOSE WHO DON'T LIKE MEAT

Some people choose not to eat meat at all. These people are called vegetarians. People who also decide not to eat any animal products are called vegans. Vegetarians and vegans must make sure that they still have plenty of protein in their diets by substituting the meat in their diet for other high protein foods.

Carbohydrates

GRAINS

GRAINS are small, hard, dry seeds. Oats, wheat and rice are all grains. Foods containing large amounts of grain are high in starch and carbohydrates. Breakfast cereals are made from grains. Some grains are ground down into flour. Flour is used to make bread and pasta, which are both high in carbohydrates. Bread comes in many forms and can be either **SAVOURY** or sweet. Pasta is used in savoury dishes, such as lasagne and spaghetti bolognese.

POTATOES

Potatoes are root vegetables that are high in carbohydrates. Because of this, they sit in the carbohydrates food group, rather than the fruits and vegetables group. Potatoes are extremely **VERSATILE** and can be cooked in may ways.

WHY EAT CARBOHYDRATES?

Eating carbohydrates is good for us because our bodies can **CONVERT** them into energy. We need energy in order to be able to keep active. Carbohydrates release their energy slowly, meaning that our bodies can be active for longer. Athletes eat carbohydrate-rich foods when they know that they have a big sporting event ahead.

PIZZA MAKES A DELICIOUS TREAT
BUT CAN BE HIGH IN FAT AND CALORIE CONTENT. CAKES, DOUGHNUTS AND BISCUITS **ARE HIGH IN SUGAR AND FAT** AND SHOULD NOT BE EATEN TOO OFTEN.

TOO MANY CARBOHYDRATES?

It is important that we do not eat too many carbohydrates. Energy that is not used up by our bodies is stored as fat, so a person who eats too many carbohydrates could become overweight. Some carbohydrates, like chips, are less healthy, as other foods, such as sugars and fats, have been added to them.

MILK AND DAIRY

WHERE DO MILK AND DAIRY PRODUCTS COME FROM?

MILK is produced by mammals to feed their young. It contains high levels of protein, fat and calcium, all of which our bodies need to develop and grow. Most of the milk that we drink comes from cows, but the milk from many different mammals is safe for human **CONSUMPTION**. Dairy products are products that have been made using milk. These include cheese, butter and yoghurt.

Products

AFTER SEVERAL MONTHS, BABIES CAN BE INTRODUCED TO SOLID FOOD. BY THE TIME THEY ARE ONE, THEY SHOULD BE EATING A BALANCED DIET.

BABY FOOD

When a new baby is born, its body is unable to digest most foods, so for the first few months it lives solely on milk. This milk can be provided by the baby's mother. Special formulas that **MIMIC** human milk can also be given to newborns. The milk contains all of the nutrients that the child needs to grow.

UNHEALTHY DAIRY

Dairy products include more ingredients than milk alone. The addition of foods such as sugars can make the products unhealthy. Milkshakes, ice cream and sweetened yoghurts should not be eaten too often because they are high in sugars.

HEALTHY DAIRY

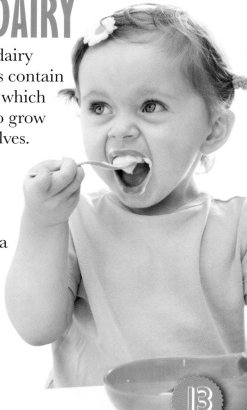

Milk and dairy products contain protein, which helps our bodies to grow and repair themselves. They also contain fat, which is good for our bodies in **MODERATION**. Milk products are a very good source of calcium, which is a mineral that helps to keep our teeth and bones strong.

FRUITS AND

WHAT IS THE DIFFERENCE BETWEEN FRUITS AND **VEGETABLES?**

MOST people believe that fruits are sweet tasting and that vegetables are more savoury. This is largely how they are sold in the supermarkets and we tend to eat them accordingly: fruit as a healthy snack or as part of a dessert, vegetables as part of a meal. Many of the foods that we call vegetables, however, are actually fruits.

FRUIT OR VEGETABLE?

Fruit is a **BOTANICAL** word which describes the part of a plant where seeds grow. Therefore, any natural food with seeds inside it is a fruit: apples, oranges, cucumbers, aubergines, pea pods, to name a few. Vegetable is a **CULINARY** word. The vegetables that we eat which are not fruits are from different parts of plants.

A CARROT IS THE TAP ROOT OF ITS PLANT AND CELERY IS THE STEM OF ITS PLANT.

Vegetables

TRY TO EAT AS MANY PORTIONS OF VEGETABLES AS YOU DO FRUITS; VEGETABLES TEND TO BE MUCH LOWER IN SUGAR!

FRUIT OR VEGETABLE: DOES IT REALLY MATTER?

In a word: no. All fruits and vegetables contain vitamins and minerals, which are important for our bodies. Vitamins are chemicals which help the body to work properly and help to prevent disease. Minerals are tiny substances that come from the soil. Calcium and iron are both minerals.

HEALTHY FRUITS AND VEGETABLES

We should all try to eat at least five portions of fruits and vegetables a day. Different fruits and vegetables contain different vitamins and minerals, so it is a good idea to vary your intake as much as possible. As well as containing vitamins and minerals, fruits and vegetables are low in fat.

FATS AND

FATS

IT is a common myth that all fats are bad for us. In reality, our bodies need a small amount of fat to be in our diets. Fat gives us energy and helps to keep our skin healthy.

As with all foods, the healthier the source of the fat, the better it is for us. One source of fat in our diets is animal fat. Sometimes the animal fat in our food is visible, but it is also found in many foods that you might not have expected it to. For this reason, vegetarians and vegans must be careful when choosing their food.

FATS CAN ALSO COME FROM PLANTS, IN THE FORM OF OILS.

UNHEALTHY FATS

A specific type of fat, known as saturated fat, is not good for our bodies and we should try to not eat too much of it. Saturated fat can make us overweight and damage our insides. It is found in foods such as processed meats, butter and lard.

Sugars

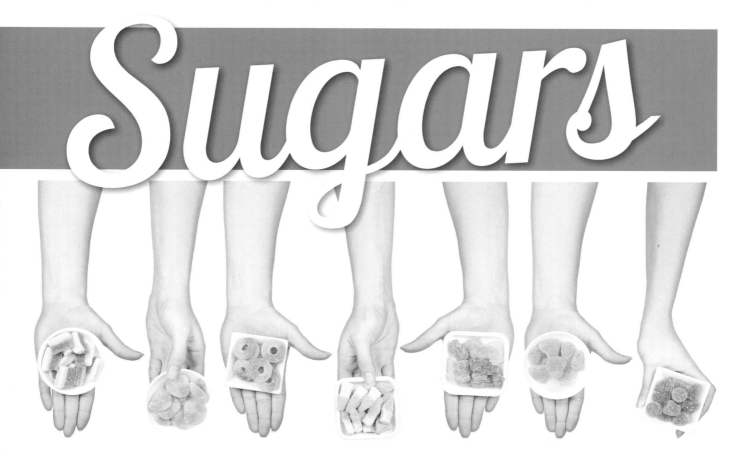

SUGARS

Sugar is a sweet substance which comes from plants. Some foods, such as fruits, are high in natural sugars. Other foods have sugar added to them.

This sugar comes from plants such as sugar cane or sugar beet and is treated to remove any **IMPURITIES**. We call this sugar refined sugar. It is added to foods to make them taste sweeter.

TOO MUCH SUGAR IN OUR DIETS, CAN LEAD TO CAVITIES

NATURAL SUGAR IS BETTER FOR US THAN REFINED SUGAR.

HIDDEN SUGARS

Some sugars are more visible than others. We know that there is sugar in sweets and fizzy drinks, but even savoury foods like soups contain refined sugar. Flavoured yoghurt, pasta sauces and even dried fruits have sugar added to them.

WATER

DRINKING WATER

WATER is an extremely important part of our diets: the human body could not live without it! Up to 60% of our bodies are made up of water, including our blood, saliva and sweat. Our bodies lose water naturally, so we need to drink fresh water every single day. The amount of water that we need to drink each day depends on many things, including our age, our gender, the weather and our activity levels.

IT IS A GOOD IDEA TO **DRINK AROUND** **2** **LITRES OF WATER** EVERY DAY.

WHAT DOES WATER DO?

Water is needed to replace the liquid that we lose through breathing, sweating and going to the toilet. It helps to digest food by moving it along the intestines. Water then travels to the blood. The kidneys remove any waste water and send it to your **BLADDER**.

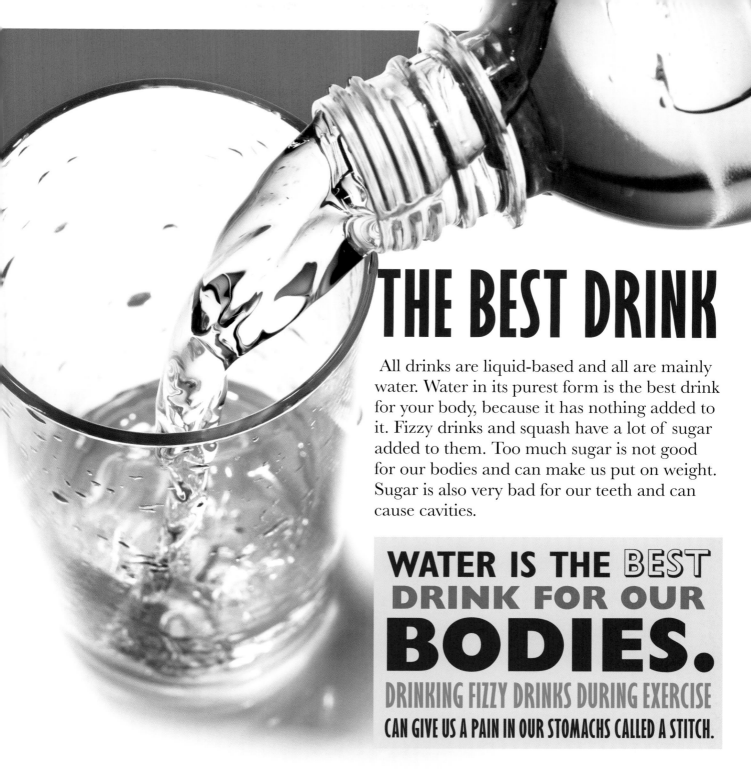

THE BEST DRINK

All drinks are liquid-based and all are mainly water. Water in its purest form is the best drink for your body, because it has nothing added to it. Fizzy drinks and squash have a lot of sugar added to them. Too much sugar is not good for our bodies and can make us put on weight. Sugar is also very bad for our teeth and can cause cavities.

WATER IS THE BEST DRINK FOR OUR BODIES.

DRINKING FIZZY DRINKS DURING EXERCISE CAN GIVE US A PAIN IN OUR STOMACHS CALLED A STITCH.

WATER AND EXERCISE

When we exercise we need to drink more water. This is because exercise causes us to lose water through breathing more quickly and sweating. It is important that we take a drink with us when we do exercise, as too little water can make us feel unwell.

THE DIGESTIVE

THE JOURNEY OF OUR FOOD

OUR bodies are designed to take in food – it is how we stay alive. Food enters our bodies through our mouths. It then makes its way through our bodies, being broken down into tiny pieces and used as the body needs. We call the body parts responsible for this, the digestive system.

THERE ARE THOUSANDS OF TASTE BUDS ON YOUR TONGUE WHICH DETECT FLAVOUR.

SMELL AND TASTE

Our sense of smell and taste help to protect us. If a food does not smell nice, you are unlikely to put it into your mouth. If you do put something into your mouth that is foul-tasting, you still have time to spit it out. Smell and taste also help to start the digestive process. If you smell something delicious, your mouth starts to produce a clear liquid called saliva. Saliva makes your food moist, which makes it easier to eat.

System

CANINES

INCISORS

MOLARS AND PRE-MOLARS

THE TEETH

Teeth have the important job of breaking down your food to manageable sizes before you swallow it. The teeth at the front of your mouth (the incisors) are designed for biting, whilst the teeth at the back of the mouth (the molars and pre-molars) are designed for chewing. Canines are the sharpest teeth, they help to tear food, such as meat.

THE TONGUE IS A POWERFUL **MUSCLE** WHICH MOVES FOOD AROUND YOUR **MOUTH, HELPING TO BREAK IT DOWN.**

THE OESOPHAGUS

When your teeth and saliva have sufficiently broken down your food, you swallow it. The tube at the back of your mouth is called the oesophagus. The walls of the oesophagus are lined with muscles which help to push the food down to the stomach.

WE ALSO BREATHE THROUGH OUR **MOUTHS. A FLAP OF SKIN** STOPS OUR FOOD TRAVELLING INTO OUR LUNGS.

❶ THE STOMACH

FOOD that has been swallowed first travels to the stomach. The stomach is like an **ELASTICATED** bag for holding food. The stomach is a small organ but it can stretch to fit a large amount of food. The muscles in the stomach **CHURN** the food and the strong acid in the stomach helps to break it down further.

❷ THE SMALL INTESTINE

Once the food leaves the stomach, it enters the small intestine. The food is broken down even more and organs such as the liver and pancreas help to digest it. After as much as ten hours, the food is finally ready to be absorbed by the body.

THE SMALL INTESTINE OF AN ADULT HUMAN CAN BE AS LONG AS 7.5 METRES!

2......

4........

3 THE LARGE INTESTINE

The food travels from the small intestine into the large intestine. The large intestine is much larger in **DIAMETER** than the small intestine, but it is nowhere near as long. The job of the large intestine is to absorb water from the remainder of the food. By the time the food has moved through the large intestine, it becomes more solid.

4 WASTE PRODUCTS

The solid mass that remains once the food has travelled through the body is not needed. It waits at the end of the large intestine, the rectum, until you go to the toilet. This waste product is called faeces.

IT TAKES FOOD BETWEEN 18 AND 36 HOURS TO TRAVEL RIGHT THROUGH THE BODY AND EXIT AS WASTE.

......3

ROTTEN FOODS

FRESH FOODS

Fresh foods, such as meat, fish and vegetables, are the healthiest for our bodies, but it is important that we only eat them when it is safe to do so. This is because fresh foods can become spoilt by germs and bacteria which are so small that we cannot see them. Fresh foods should be kept in a fridge because the cool temperatures help to stop germs spreading.

IT IS ALWAYS BEST TO WASH FRESH FOODS BEFORE YOU COOK OR EAT THEM.

AVOIDING GONE-OFF FOODS

If a food looks or smells bad, then it could be rotten, which means it is unsafe to eat. Foods like meat usually come with a **USE-BY DATE**, so always make sure you eat the food within that time. Keeping your hands and your kitchen clean when preparing food will help to stop spreading germs.

ALLERGIES

BAD REACTION

Sometimes, a person's body can react badly to a certain food. This is called an allergy. Allergies happen when the body mistakenly thinks that a food is a harmful substance. Allergic reactions can include rashes, sickness and diarrhoea. If somebody is allergic to a certain food, then they must always avoid it.

NUTS, SHELLFISH AND EGGS ARE AMONG FOODS THAT CAN CAUSE ALLERGIC REACTIONS.

LIFE-THREATENING ALLERGIES

In the worst case, allergies can be life-threatening because they can cause problems with a person's breathing. These allergies are pretty rare. If you are ever with a person who has a bad reaction to something they have eaten then you should call an ambulance. Doctors are able to treat bad allergies with special medicines.

SOME PEOPLE WITH AN ALLERGY CARRY SPECIAL MEDICINES AROUND WITH THEM FOR EMERGENCIES.

MAKING

THE BALANCED PLATE

Remember the balanced plate on page 7? This shows you the amount of each food group that you should try to eat. Try to remember that image at each meal time, so that you can make sure your diet is balanced and try to make sure that the snacks that you eat throughout the day are healthy ones, which are good for your body.

DO REMEMBER, THOUGH, IT IS OKAY TO HAVE TREATS SOMETIMES!

HOW DO WE CHOOSE?

There are so many choices when it comes to what we can eat. Supermarkets have a larger selection of food than ever before and there are more supermarkets than ever before. In towns and cities, there are new restaurants and **FAST-FOOD OUTLETS** that appear all of the time. Even in our school canteens, the choice of foods is widening all of the time – so how can we be sure that we are eating the healthiest things?

Choices

AT SCHOOL

Many children have cooked lunches from their school canteens. School dinners are healthier than they ever have been, but it is still important that you make choices that are the right ones for your body. Try to regularly change your meals at school. Some schools offer a healthy alternative to the main meal, such as a jacket potato. This is a sensible option once or twice a week, but you should try to avoid having the same thing each and every day.

SCHOOL DINNERS

If your school provides some options that are not as healthy as others, such as chips or sugary puddings, remember that it is fine to choose these options sometimes. Maybe try choosing these once or twice a week and choose desserts such as fruit or yoghurt on the other days. It is always a good idea to talk to your parents about the lunches that you choose, so that they can help you to make the healthiest decisions.

IF YOU TAKE A PACKED LUNCH INTO SCHOOL, OR SOME SNACKS **FOR BREAK TIME,** HELP YOUR PARENT TO CHOOSE WHAT **YOU TAKE IN AND** TRY TO CHOOSE HEALTHY OPTIONS.

AT HOME

The adults in our homes tend to be responsible for the types of food that we eat. As we get older, however, it is a good idea to get involved with the choosing and preparing of food. This means that you can have a say in what family meals are chosen and you can learn important skills that you will need to use later in life.

PERHAPS YOU DON'T THINK THAT YOUR EVENING MEALS AT HOME ARE HEALTHY ENOUGH. WHY NOT TALK TO YOUR PARENTS ABOUT THE BALANCED PLATE?

FAMILY MEALS

If your family already eats a balanced diet, then you will be able to learn a lot about the process of doing so. Some families tend to eat the same meals each week.

Although the meals may well be healthy, variety is still best. Why not suggest a healthy meal choice to your parents, or offer to help prepare a new meal one evening?

IN THE SUPERMARKET

With aisles and aisles filled with delicious foods, it can be easy to come out of a supermarket with lots of treats and not so many healthy meals and snacks. For this reason, it is best to plan out your meals and make a shopping list before you go. Try to help your parents write this list so that you can be involved in the choices they make.

TRY TO FILL YOUR TROLLEY
WITH ALL THE TYPES OF FOOD
ON THE BALANCED PLATE.

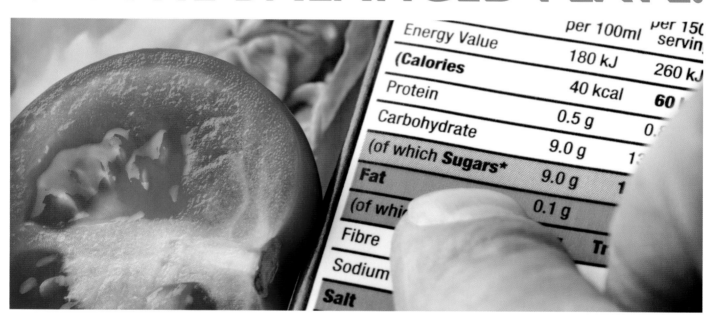

Energy Value	per 100ml	per 150 serving
(Calories	180 kJ	260 kJ
Protein	40 kcal	60
Carbohydrate	0.5 g	0.5
(of which Sugars*	9.0 g	13
Fat	9.0 g	1
(of whic	0.1 g	
Fibre		Tr
Sodium		
Salt		

FOOD LABELS

Have a look at the labels of the foods that you are choosing. They will tell you how much salt, sugar and fat there is in it. Most shops use the traffic light system to help their shoppers understand the information. Remember that green is best!

THE LESS
PREPARED
A FOOD
IS WHEN
YOU BUY IT,
THE HEALTHIER IT IS.

WITH FRIENDS

If you are eating with your friends, especially for a special occasion, remember that it is okay to have some treats. It may be that you have gone to a friend's house for dinner. It would be impolite to comment on the healthiness of a meal provided by a friend's parent. It might be that your friend's parent has chosen to prepare a meal that is a treat for you both.

PEER PRESSURE

Sometimes, we can feel pressured into doing things that we might not want to do. It might be that your friends do not eat a diet that is as healthy as yours and try to encourage you to do the same. Stay strong on these occasions and know that you are making the best choices for your body. Maybe you could offer your friends a healthier option instead?

Glossary

bladder	**the organ that holds and releases urine**
botanical	relating to the scientific study of plants
cease	**stop or bring to an end**
churn	mix around
consumption	**eating**
convert	change
culinary	**to do with cooking**
diameter	the width of an object
elasticated	**stretchy and flexible**
fast-food outlets	places that sell take-away food
fatigue	**tiredness**
impurities	parts that damage the purity of something
informed choices	**knowing all the options before you make a choice**
mimic	imitate or copy
moderation	**avoiding large amounts or excess**
savory	salty or spicy, not sweet
tap root	**the largest root of a plant, from which other roots sprout**
use-by date	date by which a food should be eaten
versatile	**able to be used in many ways**

Index

PHOTO CREDITS

Photocredits: Abbreviations: l–left, r–right, b–bottom, t–top, c–centre, m–middle. All images are courtesy of Shutterstock.com.
Front Cover – Jeka. 2 – GUNDAM_Ai. 4–5tm – jordache. 4br – Duplass. 4ml – www.BillionPhotos.com. 5br – pathdoc. 5tr – amenic181. 6ml – Oksana Kuzmina. 6–7m – ifong. 8 – www.BillionPhotos.com. 9 – Oksana Kuzmina. 10tr – Tischenko Irina. 10 – BestPhotoStudio. 11tr – Maridav. 11m – Joshua Resnick. 11br – Melica. 12lm – Elena Schweitzer. 12–13m – Guitar photographer. 14t – Lana K. 14bl – Boumen Japet. 15t – leonori. 16t – Jacek Chabraszewski. 16br – Sea Wave. 17t – 123object. 17bl – Zoroyan. 18l – MAHATHIR MOHD YASIN. 19t – artjazz. 19br – majeczka. 20t – Zurijeta. 20br – Liudmila P. Sundikova. 21t – manas_ko. 22m – Photographee.eu. 22–23m – bluezace. 23br – Luis Molinero. 24t – Anna Hoychuk. 24br – Joerg Beuge. 25tl – Skydive Erick. 25mr – Rob Byron. 26tl – ifong. 26 – 27bm – Niloo. 27tr – SpeedKingz. 28t – racorn. 28 – 29bm – Spotmatik Ltd. 29m – Brian A Jackson. 30t – Oksana Kuzmina. 30b – wong sze yuen.
Images are courtesy of Shutterstock.com. With thanks to Getty Images, Thinkstock Photo and iStockphoto.